W9-BCX-860

DATE DUE

JOHN STOCKTON

AD

ADRIAN DANTLEY

DARRELL GRIFFITH

JACQUE VAUGHN

MARK EATON

THURL BAILEY

Pistol →

The MailMan

PETE MARAVICH

KARL MALONE

LEONARD ROBINSON

JEFF HORNACEK

RICKEY GREEN

BRYON RUSSELL

CREATIVE C EDUCATION

AARON FRISCH

Published by Creative Education, 123 South Broad Street, Mankato, MN 56001

Creative Education is an imprint of The Creative Company.

Designed by Rita Marshall

Photos by Active Images, Allsport, AP/Wide World, Rich Kane, NBA Photos, SportsChrome

Library of Congress Cataloging-in-Publication Data

Frisch, Aaron. The history of the Utah Jazz / by Aaron Frisch.

p. cm. — (Pro basketball today)   ISBN 1-58341-116-X

1. Utah Jazz (Basketball team)—History—

Juvenile literature. [1. Utah Jazz (Basketball team)—History.

2. Basketball—History.] I. Title. II. Series.

GV885.52.U8 F75 2001   796.323'64'09792258—dc21   00-047333

First Edition 9 8 7 6 5 4 3 2 1

THE STATE OF UTAH IS KNOWN

AS A QUIET, RELIGIOUS REGION.

ITS CAPITAL AND LARGEST CITY—SALT LAKE CITY—

is the worldwide headquarters of the Church of Jesus Christ of Latter-day Saints, more commonly known as the Mormon Church. Utah was settled in 1847 by Mormon pioneer Brigham Young and his followers, who were trying to escape religious persecution. Today, Mormons still make up most of Utah's population.

At first glance, Salt Lake City has virtually nothing in common with New Orleans, a swinging Louisiana city known for its jazz music and many nightclubs. Yet both cities have been home to the same

E.C. COLEMAN

5

National Basketball Association (NBA) team. That team, born as the

New Orleans Jazz, moved to Utah's quiet capital in 1979 and became an

instant hit.

{THE NEW ORLEANS YEARS} The Jazz started out

in New Orleans in 1974. The team's owners were deter-

mined to make the Jazz like the city of New Orleans—

colorful and entertaining. To do this, they decked out

their team in bright uniforms of purple, green, and gold. They also

brought in one of the league's greatest showmen by trading for point

guard Pete Maravich.

Known to fans as "Pistol Pete," Maravich was a sensational player

whose speed and flair for ball handling was unmatched. "This man is

quicker and faster than [NBA stars] Jerry West or Oscar Robertson," said

Atlanta Hawks forward Lou Hudson. "He gets the ball up the floor better.

MARK EATON

Guard Pete Maravich provided plenty of high-lights during the New Orleans era.

PETE MARAVICH

He shoots as well. Raw talent-wise, he's the greatest who ever played."

As a kid, Maravich had carried a ball with him everywhere he went. Whether he was going to school or the corner store, he was always dribbling a basketball. Years later, that practice paid off. Pistol Pete controlled the ball as if it were attached to his hand by a string, and he thrilled fans with deadly long-range shooting and an array of trick passes.

The Jazz bolstered their offense by trading for All-Star guard Gail Goodrich in **1976**.

Maravich put on some great shows in New Orleans, but the team struggled, posting losing records in its first three seasons. The Jazz's best season during those years was 1975–76, when Maravich and veteran center Otto Moore led the team to a respectable 38–44 record. In 1976–77, Maravich had his best season ever, leading the NBA in scoring with 31 points per game. In one game against New York that season, Pistol Pete scored an incredible 68 points.

GAIL GOODRICH

Like Pete
Maravich,
forward
Bryon Russell
was capable
of scoring in
bunches.

BRYON RUSSELL

Unfortunately, no other Jazz player could match Maravich's hero-ics. Despite the strong play of forward Leonard "Truck" Robinson, guard

Gail Goodrich, and center Rich Kelley, the team missed the playoffs again in both 1978 and 1979. A knee injury had slowed Maravich down, and New Orleans fans grew impatient with the struggling team. With attendance at home games terribly low, the team's owners decided to

move the Jazz to Salt Lake City in 1979.

{DANTLEY FINDS A HOME IN UTAH} The people of Utah were no strangers to professional basketball. In the late 1960s and early '70s, Salt Lake City had been home to the Utah Stars of the American Basketball Association (ABA)—a team that featured some of the league's top players. When the ABA began to struggle, the Stars franchise folded in 1975. Four years later, Utah fans were thrilled to welcome the Jazz to town.

LEONARD ROBINSON

The Jazz were determined to get off to a better start in Utah than they had in New Orleans. To do that, the team made several key moves. Tom Nissalke was hired as head coach, and Frank Layden—a big man

known for his sense of humor—was named the team's new general manager. One of Layden's first moves was to trade forward Spencer Haywood to the Los Angeles Lakers for 6-foot-5 forward Adrian Dantley.

Dantley had been named the NBA Rookie of the Year in 1977, and

in the seasons that followed, he established himself as one of the

league's top scorers. Yet strangely, he had been traded

year after year; Utah was Dantley's fourth home in four

years. Coach Nissalke, however, was confident that Utah

would keep Dantley for some time. "There's no one play-

er in the league who has shown me yet he can handle

14 Dantley," Nissalke said. "A.D.'s just so strong. You can't stop him inside."

No one could stop Dantley in 1979–80, as the forward led the

Jazz with 28 points per game and was named an NBA All-Star. After the

season, Utah made another major roster change. Having decided to place

their future on Dantley's broad shoulders, the Jazz released Maravich.

Years later, Pistol Pete would be inducted into the Hall of Fame.

Dantley continued to excel over the next two years, leading the

ADRIAN DANTLEY

NBA in scoring in 1980–81 and coming close the next season. The team

also got a boost from high-flying young guard Darrell Griffith, who

boasted a deadly outside shot. As Layden once said, "Griffith could

shoot from the shores of the Great Salt Lake and probably make it."

Despite Dantley and Griffith's best efforts, the Jazz continued to lose.

In 1981, Nissalke was fired as head coach and replaced by Layden.

The change seemed to be just the spark the young Jazz needed. In

1983–84, they soared to a 45–37 record and made the playoffs for the

first time. Dantley again led the NBA in scoring, but he had

plenty of help. Griffith continued his hot shooting, point

guard Rickey Green led the league in steals, and 7-foot-4

center Mark Eaton swatted away an NBA-high 351 shots.

These players led Utah to solid records again the

next two seasons, but they never truly contended for the league champi-

onship. In the NBA Draft in 1984 and 1985, however, the Jazz found

two players who would make Utah a force. Those players were point

guard John Stockton and forward Karl Malone.

{"THE MAILMAN" DELIVERS} Of the two new additions,

Malone had the quicker impact. At 6-foot-9 and a chiseled 255 pounds,

Malone was extremely powerful, yet he was also exceptionally graceful.

> Pouring in 22 points a game, Darrell Griffith emerged as Utah's top scorer in **1982–83**.

DARRELL GRIFFITH

"The Mailman," Karl Malone, was nearly unstoppable when he attacked the basket.

Fans called him "the Mailman," because no matter what the team

needed—be it a clutch basket or rebound—he always delivered. Malone

also delivered excitement in Utah, often finishing fast

breaks with a thunderous dunk. "People tend to get out

of Karl's way unless they want their careers to be over,"

Green explained.

In 1986, the Jazz decided to make Malone their

cornerstone player and traded Dantley to Detroit. The Mailman imme-

diately assumed command in Utah, leading the team with 21 points and

10 rebounds per game in 1986–87. He also continued to earn accolades

from players and coaches around the league. "He runs the court like a

small man, then overpowers bigger people," said Golden State Warriors

coach Don Nelson. "Is there a more dominant power forward in the

game today? If there is, I'd like to see him."

THURL BAILEY

Relentless guard John Stockton led the NBA in assists for nine seasons in a row.

JOHN STOCKTON

for a championship. But Utah only grew stronger. In 1996–97, the

Mailman poured in 27 points per game and was named the NBA's Most

Valuable Player, and the Jazz soared to a 64–18 record—

their best mark ever. In the playoffs, they crushed the

Clippers and Lakers to reach the Western Conference

Finals. This time, the Jazz would not be denied, beating a

tough Houston team to advance to the NBA Finals at last.

Antoine Carr teamed up with Karl Malone to give Utah an imposing frontcourt tandem.

In the Finals, the Jazz faced the mighty Chicago Bulls and star

guard Michael Jordan. The Bulls won the first two games, but Utah bat-

tled back to even the series at two games apiece. Stockton and Malone

repeatedly ran their trademark pick and roll play, and young players

such as forward Bryon Russell, center Greg Ostertag, and swingman

Shandon Anderson made big contributions as well. Unfortunately,

Jordan dominated in the next two games to lead Chicago to its second

ANTOINE CARR

straight NBA championship.

A year later, Utah charged right back to the same position, meeting

the Bulls in the NBA Finals. Unfortunately for Jazz fans,

the result was also the same. With Utah on the ropes in

game six, Malone scored 31 points. Jordan was even better,

however, netting 45 points in the final game of his career

to give Chicago the championship again.

{THE JAZZ PLAY ON} After losing in the Finals for the second

straight year, many fans wondered if Utah would replace Stockton or

Malone with younger talent while the veterans still had trade value. But

Jazz president Frank Layden made clear that he intended to keep the

team's veterans together for as long as it took. "We want to have statues

of John and Karl outside the Delta Center someday," he said.

"You'll never see us panic or make changes just to make changes.

GREG OSTERTAG

We do things differently here."

Malone proved that age had not slowed him by winning the

league's MVP award again in 1998–99. His teammates

also continued to perform at a consistently high level.

Stockton's constant hustle paced the offense, Ostertag

emerged as one of the NBA's top shot blockers, Hornacek

and Russell provided steady scoring, and Anderson and

guard Howard Eisley gave the team great bench support.

As the team's sixth man in **1999–00**, guard Howard Eisley dealt out four assists a game.

Still, the Jazz couldn't quite get back to the NBA Finals. After

posting great records, they fell to the Portland Trail Blazers in the sec-

ond round of the playoffs in both 1999 and 2000. Despite the setbacks,

Malone asked Jazz fans not to lose hope. "As long as I'm here and

Stockton's here and . . . the young guys and Jerry Sloan are here, I don't

think this [was] our last chance," he said.

HOWARD EISLEY

Multitalented forward Donyell Marshall emerged as a key rebounder in **2000–01**.

DONYELL MARSHALL

Fans expected Jacque Vaughn to succeed Stockton as the team's point guard.

JACQUE VAUGHN

For years, the Jazz have been the image of team unity. In an era

when many NBA teams shuffle their rosters almost yearly, Utah has

built a legacy of winning basketball by staying loyal to its players and its

fans. To such a team and community, a long-awaited NBA championship

would be sweet music indeed.